Finding GOD in Ordinary Things

A 30-DAY DEVOTIONAL TO CONNECT YOU WITH GOD

Kathleen Trock-Molhoek
Illustrations by Elizabeth Visser

PRAYERSHOP
PUBLISHING

Terre Haute, Indiana

PrayerShop Publishing is the publishing arm of the Church Prayer Leaders Network. The Church Prayer Leaders Network exists to equip and inspire local churches and their prayer leaders in their desire to disciple their people in prayer and to become a "house of prayer for all nations." Its online store, prayershop.org, has more than 150 prayer resources available for purchase or download.

ISBN: 978-1-935012-95-5

1 2 3 4 5 | 2024 2023 2022 2021 2020

ACKNOWLEDGMENTS

Looking at the first journal entries for this devotional, I am reminded of those who have walked alongside me with words of encouragement and prayers.

I wish to thank:

my husband, Dan, for his encouragement, patience, and editing.

my children, Jennifer and Alex, who provided me with the inspiration for this devotional. Looking into their eyes when they were children, I longed to find a way to tell them about Jesus in a way they would *know* Him, not just stories *about* Him. Through *Finding God in Ordinary Things*, I hope others will experience "knowing God" as they do.

Ginny Emery, my prayer partner and friend, for her continual belief that there are books in me that need to be written.

The Potters House School in Grand Rapids, Michigan, under their spiritual director, Dr. Antonio Tendero, and teachers EunSub Cho, Aubrey Cantrell, Jeanne Smith, and their students who read through the devotionals and offered valuable insights.

I am also thankful for Sandy Smith, Pebbles and Stones administrator, along with Raina Daily, Esther Uitvlught, Rehanna Pitch, Adrienne Niswander, and others for their encouragement and editing.

And thank you, Jonathan Graf and PrayerShop Publishing, for seeing the value of this devotional.

TABLE OF CONTENTS

INTRODUCTION

Thank you for picking-up *Finding God in Ordinary Things*. It was written for you.

Years ago, I developed a way to look at ordinary things and to see how they remind me of God.

I began by reflecting on something that caught my attention during the day. It could be anything from a drop of water to a stone.

Second, I tried to think of a Bible verse about it. If I couldn't come up with one, I did a word search on my computer. For example, in searching for "stone--Bible Verse," one of the verses that came up was 1 Peter 2:5 "You yourselves like living stones are being built up as a spiritual house, to be a holy priesthood, to offer spiritual sacrifices acceptable to God through Jesus Christ."

Third, I connected the verse with something that was familiar to me, for example, using stones to build a fort. I thought about how important it was to place the right stones in the right places to make the walls strong.

Fourth, I searched for a Bible story that further connected the verse for me. For example, Peter wasn't really talking about stones; stones were metaphors for people building the church. So, I looked for a Bible story about people gathering and found Acts 2:1-21. In this passage believers in the early church met in one place and were in one accord as they waited for the day of Pentecost.

Fifth, I asked myself questions about the verse and Bible story. For example, "What do these verses tell me about God? What does it mean that God has called me a "living stone? Why does it matter who I hang out with? How should I relate to other people?"

Sixth, from my reflections, I wrote a prayer and/or drew a prayer picture.

You hold in your hand thirty days of seeing ordinary things as connectors to God.

This devotional is set up using that model. Each day you will read about an ordinary thing, and explore what it tells you about God.

Then at the end of the book, I give you the same model used throughout the devotional so you can begin writing your own devotionals. My prayer is that as you write, you will continue to see how God can use ordinary things to remind you of Him throughout the day.

DAY
1

First clean the inside
of the cup and dish,
and then the outside
will also be clean.

MATTHEW 23:26

DIRT

What is the hardest thing for you to clean?

Glancing around to be sure no one was looking, Eric quickly finished sweeping dirt under the rug. He thought to himself: *No one will know that I didn't finish my job, and besides, I don't want to be late for the movie with my friends.* Eric guessed correctly; his mother didn't notice the dirt under the rug. She commended Eric for finishing his work before going to the movies. Eric's head swelled with pride. He loved praise, and he felt smug fooling his mother.

One day, Jesus noticed similar behavior with the Pharisees. Jews recognized these leaders as upright and devoted to teaching and knowing the law of God. Some of them were faithful, but many in Jesus' day lived just like Eric. They loved acknowledgment by the people and appearing like they were righteous (doing the right things), but their hearts strayed far from God.

In the Book of Matthew, Jesus explained that God the Father looks at the heart, not the outward appearance of people. Jesus stood among the crowds, teachers, and disciples, saying, "The teachers of the law and the Pharisees sit in Moses' seat. So, you must be careful to do everything they tell you. But do not do what they do, for they do not practice what they preach" (Mt. 23:2-4).

Jesus wasn't frustrated that Pharisees knew the law or even quoted it. His problem focused on how they pretended to do it (hypocrisy). He felt troubled that they didn't understand the laws about loving God, loving others, showing mercy, and obeying Him. The Pharisees cared more about appearances than obeying the Lord.

Getting Clean on the Inside

1. "If we confess our sins, He is faithful and just to forgive us our sins and to cleanse us from all unrighteousness" (1 Jn. 1:9, KJV). Based on this scripture, how do we become clean on the inside?

2. How can you apply Eric's story to your life?

3. Write a prayer or draw a prayer picture based on what God spoke to you about today's verse, and your answers to the questions.

Read more about getting clean and truly loving others at
Matthew 5:20 • Matthew 7:4-5 • Luke 6:31-36 • Mathew 23:5-7

DAY 2

Can any one of you by worrying add a single hour to your life?

MATTHEW 6:27

BIRDS

What does your favorite outfit look like?

Tanisha loved birds and enjoyed going to the zoo to see exotic ones. She marveled at the bright colors of the Toucan, the Paradise Tanager, and the Spoonbill. Her favorite bird was the Macaw. Its bright colors reminded her of her favorite scarf that she had lost. She thought she might have left it at school, but worried that it might not be there.

Jesus understands our tendency to worry, about lost scarves, as well as difficult friendships, looming homework and more. One day, as Jesus was teaching, He wanted His listeners to understand that He would provide for them and for them not to worry. He said to them, "Look at the birds of the air; they do not sow or reap or store away in barns, and yet your heavenly Father feeds them. Are you not much more valuable than they? Can any one of you by worrying add a single hour to your life?" . . . Your Father who is in heaven knows that you need them. . . . But seek first his kingdom and his righteousness, and all these things will be given to you as well. Therefore do not worry about tomorrow" (Matthew 6:26-34).

When we don't have something we want, our first response might be to worry, as Tanisha did after losing her scarf. In this passage, Jesus tells us to do something different. He tells us to look around and see how God takes care of the birds, flowers, and grass. He promises us that God our Father will provide even more for us when we put Him first (seek His Kingdom first).

Your Worry, God's Care

1. How do you act when you feel worried?

2. Based on this scripture passage, why would seeking God's Kingdom first help you not to worry? Matthew 6:26-34.

3. Write a prayer or draw a prayer picture based on today's scripture verse, devotional reading, and your answers to the questions.

Read more about your worry and God's care at
John 14:1 • Philippians 4:6 • 1 Peter 5:7

DAY 3

WORLD MAP

Then I heard the voice of the Lord saying, "Whom shall I send? And who will go for us?" And I said, "Here am I. Send me!"

ISAIAH 6:8

What country would you like to visit? What would you like to see and do there?

"What is the capital of Burundi?" Daniel asked his class. Before anyone could answer, he shouted, "Bujumbura!"

Daniel continued to ask other questions like, "What is the capital of Swaziland? Lobamba! What is the capital of Botswana? Gaborone!"

Daniel loved learning about countries. He focused on the world map hanging in the classroom, and spouted off the names of the countries and their capitals, until his teacher asked him to stop, allowing other students to participate in the geography lesson. In his alone time, Daniel dreamed of visiting all the countries in the world.

Even more than Daniel, God knows the names of all the countries and their capitals, and He also knows the names of everyone who lives in them. He created each person to know Him. The apostle Paul, in Romans 10:14, asked, "How, then, can they call on the one they have not believed in? And how can they believe in the one of whom they have not heard? And how can they hear without someone preaching to them?" He wanted the whole world to know about Jesus, and for believers to travel and share the Good News about Him.

One of the first stories about a believer telling someone about Jesus appears in the book of John. After Jesus called Andrew to be His disciple, Andrew immediately found his brother Simon and told him, "We have found the Messiah" (Jn. 1:41b).

After Jesus trained His disciples, He sent them out to tell others saying, "Therefore go and make disciples of all nations, baptizing them in the name of the Father and of the Son and of the Holy Spirit, and teaching them to obey everything I have commanded you. And surely I am with you always, to the very end of the age" (Mt. 28:19-20).

Going Into Your World

1. Who was the first person to tell you about Jesus? What was your response?

_____

_____

_____

2. Take a few minutes to ask the Lord to show you someone who needs to hear about Jesus. Who is it?

_____

_____

_____

3. Write a prayer or draw a prayer picture based on today's scripture verse, devotional, and your answers to the questions.

Learn more about sharing the Gospel of Jesus at
Isaiah 6:8 • Mark 16:15 • Acts 1:8

DAY 4

CELL PHONES

Call to me and I will answer you and tell you great and unsearchable things you do not know.

JEREMIAH 33:3

When do you urgently want someone to talk to?

Jamie jammed the cell phone into his pocket.

He grumbled, "Not picking up again. Why? Why? Why? I need to talk, and I need to talk now!" This was not the first time Jamie needed someone to talk to—a friend who would listen and give advice.

Unlike Jamie's friend, God is always present with us and hears when we call out to Him.

The Bible records the story of Peter and John, disciples of Jesus, who called on Him for help during a tough time. Government officials threw them into prison for telling others about Jesus and healing a crippled man. These disciples created such a stir, the leaders of Jerusalem met together to decide how they could stop Peter and John from talking about Jesus.

The leaders asked these disciples, "How is this crippled man now able to walk?" Peter and John answered, "... It is by the name of Jesus Christ of Nazareth, whom you crucified but whom God raised from the dead, that this man stands before you healed" (Acts 4:10b).

After talking together, the leaders ordered them not to speak any more in the name of Jesus. "But Peter and John replied, 'Which is right in God's eyes: to listen to you, or to him? You be the judges! As for us, we cannot help speaking about what we have seen and heard.' After further threats, the leaders let them go. They could not decide how to punish them, because the people were praising God for what had happened" (Acts 4:19-21).

The disciples returned to their friends and called out to God, saying, "'Now, Lord, consider their threats and enable your servants to speak your word with great boldness. Stretch out your hand to heal and perform signs and wonders through the name of your holy servant Jesus.' After they prayed, the place where they were meeting was shaken. And they were all filled with the Holy Spirit and spoke the word of God boldly" (Acts 4:29-31).

Talking to the Lord

1. Write about a time when you needed to talk to someone, but like Jamie, nobody was available.

2. How could you apply the story of Peter and John to your life?

3. Write a prayer or draw a prayer picture based on what God spoke to you about today's verse, and your answers to the question.

Read more about how God hears you at
Psalm 34:17 • Psalm 57:2 • Psalm 77:1 • Acts 4:29-31

WATER

When do you get thirsty?

Sabra finished her first 5k run. Hot, tired, and thirsty, she walked to the refreshment stand, grabbed a bottle of water, and gulped it down. Feeling refreshed, she joined her teammates to cheer on the other runners.

Like Sabra, who was thirsty after her 5K, Jesus grew thirsty while traveling through a land called Samaria. He stopped by a well in the city of Sychar. A woman also approached the well to fill her water jugs.

"When [the] Samaritan woman came near to draw water, Jesus said to her, 'Will you give me a drink?' (His disciples had gone into the town to buy food.) The Samaritan woman said to him, 'You are a Jew and I am a Samaritan woman. How can you ask me for a drink?' (For Jews do not associate with Samaritans.) Jesus answered her, 'If you knew the gift of God and who it is that asks you for a drink, you would have asked him and he would have given you living water.'

"'Sir,' the woman said, 'you have nothing to draw with and the well is deep. Where can you get this living water? Are you greater than our father Jacob, who gave us the well and drank from it himself, as did also his sons and his livestock?'

"Jesus answered, 'Everyone who drinks this water will be thirsty again, but whoever drinks the water I give them will never thirst. Indeed, the water I give them will become in them a spring of water welling up to eternal life'" (Jn. 4:7-14).

Answering the woman, Jesus said that just as the body thirsts for water, our spirits thirst to know God. As we get to know Him, we become springs of water to refresh ourselves and others.

Do You Thirst for God?

1. When have you longed for God?

2. What do you do—or could you do—when you feel thirsty for God?

3. Write a prayer or draw a prayer picture based on today's scripture verse, devotional, and your answers to the questions.

> Read more about thirsting for God at
> Psalm 23:1-2 • Psalm 143:6 • Isaiah 58:11

COINS

In the same way,
I tell you, there is
rejoicing in the
presence of the angels
of God over one
sinner who repents.

LUKE 15:10

Have you ever saved money for something special? What was it? How long did it take you to save the money?

Micah took his money out of a box and counted it. He'd finally saved enough to buy a drone! He thought of the fun he would enjoy with it. He especially couldn't wait to use the drone to take pictures of the pond behind his house.

As Micah finished counting, he realized some money was missing. He froze as his heart started to race. *Where was it? What happened to it?* Immediately he searched and didn't stop until he discovered it under the box. Excitedly, he ran to tell his mother how he lost and then found the lost money!

Jesus told a parable about a woman who, like Micah, saved money to buy something special. She had ten coins. One night, as she counted her coins, she realized one was missing. Quickly, she swept the floor in search of the coin. She looked and looked until she found it. When she discovered the coin, she called all her neighbors together to celebrate with her.

Jesus finished the parable by saying, "In the same way, I tell you, there is rejoicing in the presence of the angels of God over one sinner who repents" (Lk. 15:10).

Repentance is the act of turning from our own way and following God's way. For example, after telling a lie, it can seem easier to keep going with it than to confess that we lied. Admitting to a lie can be challenging for many reasons. But how does God respond to us when we confess? God uses the example of the woman with the coin to show us: He rejoices!

From Sin to Repentance

1. How do you feel when you've sinned?

    _____

    _____

    _____

    _____

    _____

2. Reflect on and write about a time when you repented.

    _____

    _____

    _____

    _____

    _____

3. Write a prayer or draw a prayer picture based on what God spoke to you about today's verse, and your answers to the questions.

> Read more about repentance at
> Luke 5:32 • 2 Peter 3:9 • I John 1:9

DAY 7

The seven priests carrying the seven trumpets went forward, marching before the ark of the Lord and blowing the trumpets.

JOSHUA 6:13

TRUMPET

What is your favorite musical instrument?

Marissa looked forward to getting her first musical instrument. She had chosen the trumpet. She loved the sounds of the notes and felt they called her to action. She especially anticipated playing in the school band during football games and cheering for her team with trumpet sounds.

Many musical instruments appear in the Bible. One of them is the trumpet. Joshua used trumpets in the Battle of Jericho. Before the conflict, the city of Jericho was well secured and seemingly impenetrable. "Now the gates of Jericho were securely barred because of the Israelites. No one went out and no one came in" (Josh. 6:1).

When Joshua neared Jericho, the Lord said to him, "See, I have delivered Jericho into your hands, along with its king and its fighting men. March around the city once with all the armed men. Do this for six days. Have seven priests carry trumpets of rams' horns in front of the ark. On the seventh day, march around the city seven times, with the priests blowing the trumpets. When you hear them sound a long blast on the trumpets, have the whole army give a loud shout; then the wall of the city will collapse and the army will go up, everyone straight in" (Josh. 6:2-5).

God's battle plan for Jericho was unusual, but Joshua obeyed the Lord, and the Lord did what He said He would do. He gave the city of Jericho to Joshua.

Marissa hoped the sound of her band would encourage her team to win, but whoever heard of marching around a city for six days, blowing trumpets on the seventh day, and shouting to win a battle? It worked because God formed the battle plan and Joshua followed it. This biblical story isn't just about blowing trumpets. It's about hearing God's voice and obeying it.

Following God's Plan for You

1. How do you think Joshua felt when the Lord gave him the battle plan?

   _____

   _____

2. Has God ever given you an unusual plan? What was it? How did you respond?

   _____

   _____

3. Write a prayer or draw a prayer picture based on today's scripture verse, devotional, and your answers to the questions.

Think more about obeying God at
Deuteronomy 13:4 • Luke 11:28 • Matthew 7:24

See, I have placed before you an open door that no one can shut.

REVELATION 3:8A

DOORS

Have you ever had trouble opening door?

Henri walked around his house several times, looking for an open door. He felt flustered, knowing he had just a few minutes to get into the house and change into his hockey uniform. He vowed he would never forget his key again, as he waited for his mother to drive home.

Just as Henri got upset when he couldn't get into his house, we can grow agitated when it seems like the doors to our plans are locked. The book of Revelation states this about the Lord and doors: "What he opens no one can shut, and what he shuts no one can open" (Rev 3:7b). Many Bible characters walked through doors (opportunities) only God could have unlocked for them, or were stopped by Him from going through other doors.

As an example, Paul encountered both open and closed doors. Paul and his companions traveled through the area of Phrygia and Galatia, preaching the Gospel. On one occasion, they were "kept by the Holy Spirit from preaching the word in the province of Asia. When they came to the border of Mysia, they tried to enter Bithynia, but the Spirit of Jesus would not allow them to. So they passed by Mysia and went down to Troas. During the night Paul had a vision of a man of Macedonia standing and begging him, 'Come over to Macedonia and help us.' After Paul had seen the vision, [he] got ready at once to leave for Macedonia, concluding that God had called [him] to preach the gospel to them" (Acts 16: 6b-10).

Paul and his companions could have become flustered, like Henri, when the Holy Spirit stopped them from preaching the Gospel in Asia Minor. But they didn't. They recognized God's voice and stepped out into faith and followed, even if it meant changing directions.

To know what doors God has opened or closed will require you, like Paul, to recognize God's voice and step out in faith, into what He plans for you.

Going Through God's Doors

1. There is a familiar saying, "When God closes a door, He opens another." Have you experienced that in your life? When?

2. Is there a door you're waiting to go through? What is it? How will you know if God says yes or no to entering it?

3. Write a prayer or draw a prayer picture based on today's scripture verse, devotional, and your answers to the questions.

Think more about God's doors at
Isaiah 22:22 • 1 Corinthians 16:9 • Revelation 3:20

DAY 9

They will be called oaks of righteousness, a planting of the LORD for the display of his splendor.

ISAIAH 61:3B

TREES

What do you know about trees?

My ninety-nine-year-old mother loves trees. When I was a young girl, she often took me for walks in my grandfather's woods. On numerous walks, she identified the different trees for me and talked about each one. She taught me how to identify trees by looking at their bark, leaves, and shapes.

On one of our walks, I picked up an acorn, took it home, and planted it. The acorn sprouted and grew into a huge oak tree, gracing my mother's home with its shady branches. When the tree was young, I could have easily pulled it out by its roots.

In the Bible, the oak tree symbolizes strength. Many Bible characters stood tall like oak trees, especially David. The Philistine army gathered to fight against Israel. Goliath, a giant who measured over nine feet, mocked and challenged the Israelites for 40 days. He asked them to send one man to fight him. He said, "If he is able to fight and kill me, we will become your subjects; but if I overcome him and kill him, you will become our subjects and serve us" (1 Sam. 17:9).

When David heard this, he stood up to Goliath like a strong oak tree, convinced that God would fight for him.

Goliath saw David coming and said, "Am I a dog, that you come at me with sticks?" (1 Sam. 17:43a).

David said to the huge Philistine, "You come against me with sword and spear and javelin, but I come against you in the name of the LORD

Almighty, the God of the armies of Israel, whom you have defied. This day the LORD will deliver you into my hands, ... and the whole world will know that there is a God in Israel. All those gathered here will know that it is not by sword or spear that the LORD saves; for the battle is the LORD's, and he will give all of you into our hands" (1 Sam. 17:45-47).

So, David standing tall as a mighty oak tree, used a slingshot and a stone to kill Goliath.

Standing Tall with the Lord

1. When have you stood like a tall oak tree? Describe it.

2. When weren't you able to stand like an oak tree? What happened?

3. Write a prayer or draw a prayer picture based on today's scripture verse, devotional, and your answers to the questions.

Consider standing spiritually strong at
Psalm 52:8 • Psalm 92:12 • 1 Corinthians 16:13

DAY 10

FIRE

What would you use to start a fire?

Amanda liked the smoky smell, crackling sounds, flickering light, and warmth of her campfire. It was the first fire she made by herself for her outdoor camping club. As others gathered around the fire, they talked about what they needed to start a fire. Everyone laughed when one of the campers jokingly said, "Water."

No one would think of using water to build a fire, would they? Contrary to our ideas, that's what the prophet Elijah used.

The wicked King Ahab ruled Israel and had turned the hearts of the people to worship a pagan God, Baal. Elijah stood before the people and asked, "How long will you waver between two opinions? If the LORD is God, follow him; but if Baal is God, follow him" (1 K. 18:21).

This question resulted in a contest between Elijah and Ahab's prophets to see whose god was the One and Only True God. The rules were simple: each one would call on the name of their god after preparing a burnt sacrifice. The god who answered by fire would be the True God. Both Elijah and Ahab's prophets gathered what they needed to start the fire.

The prophets of Baal prayed first. After they piled their wood, they prayed to Baal for hours to light the fire, but nothing happened. Elijah encouraged them to shout louder and teasingly said their god might be sleeping. Even though Baal's prophets yelled and prayed to their god, the fire didn't start.

During Elijah's turn, he asked some people to pour water over the wood. Then "Elijah stepped forward and prayed, 'LORD, the God of

Abraham, Isaac, and Israel, let it be known today that you are God in Israel … Answer me, LORD, answer me, so these people will know that you, LORD, are God, and that you are turning their hearts back again.'

"Then the fire of the LORD fell and burned up the sacrifice, the wood, the stones, and the soil, and also licked up the water in the trench. When all the people saw this, they fell prostrate and cried, 'The LORD–He is God! The LORD–He is God!'" (1 K. 18:36b-39).

Your Amazing God

1. Has anyone ever challenged you for your belief in God? How did you respond?

2. Write about a time when you felt amazed by something God did.

3. Write a prayer or draw a prayer picture based on today's scripture verse, devotional, and your answers to the questions.

Think more about belonging to God at
2 Samuel 7:22   Psalm 100:3 • Isaiah 25:1

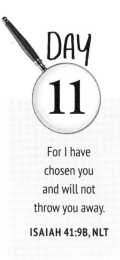

For I have
chosen you
and will not
throw you away.

ISAIAH 41:9B, NLT

TRASH CAN

Have you ever chosen or bought something and then ended up throwing it away? What was it? Why did you throw it away?

Erin slipped on her favorite shirt. As she bent over to tie her shoe, the shirt ripped down the back seam. It ripped in a way she couldn't fix it.

"Ugh! I'll need to throw it away," she lamented. "Now I need to find something else to wear to the party." As if her day wasn't already going badly! At the party, she would face her former friends who thought she wasn't good enough for them. As she threw her shirt into the garbage bin, she thought, *I feel trashed, too.*

Most of us can probably remember a time when we chose something, but ended up throwing it away, for one reason or another. I think it's safe to say we all experience times when we feel like we've been rejected or thrown away. Unlike Erin's friends, God promises He will never trash us.

The Bible tells a story about a boy named Joseph whose ten brothers threw him away. While still a child, Joseph lost his mother, probably to an illness. Joseph became his father's favorite, and his older brothers turned angry and jealous of him. One night, God gave Joseph a strange dream. He dreamed many people considered him important. So much so, his brothers and father bowed down to him in honor. Joseph excitedly told them about the dream, but it didn't go over well. Instead, his brothers' hate grew so much, they planned a time to kill him.

However, when the time arrived, the brothers ended up throwing their youngest brother into a pit and selling him as a slave instead. But even while foreigners carried Joseph away from his family into a dangerous land, God didn't leave him. God watched over Joseph and fulfilled the dream.

Just as God had a purpose, plan, and destiny for Joseph, He's also created a plan for you. When others become jealous of you, or decide not to like you for unknown reasons, hold on to God's plan for you.

God's Plan for You

1. When have you felt rejected by others? How did you handle it?

2. What plans do you think God holds for you? How could those plans help you the next time you feel rejected?

3. Write a prayer or draw a prayer picture based on today's scripture verse, devotional, and your answers to the questions.

Bask in God's acceptance at
Isaiah 41:13 • Romans 8:31-39 • 1 John 3:1

DAY 12

"Come, follow me,"
Jesus said,
"and I will send you
out to fish for people"

MATTHEW 4:19

FISHING NET

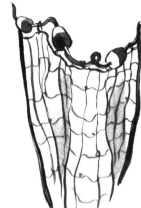

What skills do you think a fisherman needs to succeed?

David loved to fish. He imagined fishing, read about it, and understood the importance of using the right kind of bait. David knew the great places to fish and the best times to go fishing.

Like David, several of the men Jesus called to be His disciples liked to fish. In fact, they fished for a living. They also knew where and when to fish.

One day after a crowd gathered to hear Jesus teach, He said to Simon, a fisherman,

"Put out into deep water, and let down the nets for a catch."

Simon answered, "Master, we've worked hard all night and haven't caught anything. But because you say so, I will let down the nets."

When they had done so, they caught such a large number of fish that their nets began to break. So they signaled their partners in the other boat to come and help them, and they came and filled both boats so full that they began to sink.

When Simon Peter saw this, he fell at Jesus' knees and said, "Go away from me, Lord; I am a sinful man!" For he and all of his companions were astonished at the catch of fish they had taken, and so were James and John, the sons of Zebedee, Simon's partners.

Then Jesus said to Simon, "Don't be afraid; from now on you will fish for people." So, they pulled their boats up on shore, left everything and followed him (Lk. 5:4-11). ✦

Peter and his partners left their fishing jobs to follow Jesus. In years to come, they fished for people by sharing the gospel and doing signs and wonders in the name of Jesus.

Telling People about Jesus

1. How do you feel about spiritually fishing for people?

2. Have you ever told anyone about Jesus? If so, what happened?

3. Write a prayer or draw a prayer picture based on what God spoke to you about today's verse, and your answers to the questions.

Think about sharing the Good News at
Luke 2:10-12 • Acts 2:38 • Romans 10:14-15

TABLET

"...the word is very near you; it is in your mouth and in your heart so you may obey it."

DEUTERONOMY 30:14

What are some things you write down to remember?

Bradley finished writing out his history assignment in his notepad and left for his soccer practice. His team would play in the final games to determine the state championship. He paid close attention to his coach, who reviewed the plays for his team. The coach had thought through these plays carefully, and remembering them could determine the game's outcome. After practice, Bradley entered the plays into his notepad. He studied them repeatedly, until he knew them. Bradley understood how important the plays were for his team.

Similarly, God gave commandments to help us live a full life. Bradley wrote the game plays in his notebook. God wants us to keep His commands in our hearts. Speaking to the Israelites, Moses said:

These are the commands, decrees and laws the Lord your God directed me to teach you to observe in the land that you are crossing the Jordan to possess, so that you, your children and their children after them may fear the Lord your God as long as you live by keeping all his decrees and commands that I give you, and so that you may enjoy long life … Hear, O Israel: The Lord our God, the Lord is one. Love the Lord your God with all your heart and with all your soul and with all your strength. These commandments that I give you today are to be on your hearts. Impress them on your children. Talk about them when you sit at home and when you walk along the road, when you lie down and when you get up. Tie them as symbols on your hands and bind them on your foreheads. Write them on the doorframes of your houses and on your gates (Deut. 6:1-9). ✦

In the New Testament, the Scribes and Pharisees questioned Jesus about the laws. One of them asked, "'Teacher, which is the greatest commandment of the Law?' Jesus replied: 'Love the LORD your God with all your heart and with all your soul and with all your mind.' This is the first and greatest commandment. And the second is like it: 'Love your neighbor as yourself ...'" (Mt. 22:36-40).

Remembering the Commandments

1. What helps you remember God's commandments?

2. How can you love your neighbor as yourself?

3. Write a prayer or draw a prayer picture based on today's scripture verse, devotional, and your answers to the questions.

Remember the commandment about love at
Matthew 5:44 • Romans 12:10 • 1 John 4:8

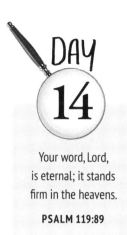

DAY
14

Your word, Lord,
is eternal; it stands
firm in the heavens.

PSALM 119:89

FLOWERS

Have you ever wished something could last forever? What was it?

For her birthday, Sarah received her first bouquet of flowers. She loved the delicate fragrance, soft touch, and vibrant colors. Sarah took good care of her flowers by adding fresh water and preservative to the vase. Unfortunately, by the end of the week, the flowers wilted and dropped their beautiful scalloped petals.

Sarah hoped the flowers would last forever, but they didn't. *Is there anything that will last forever?* she wondered. Isaiah 40:8 answers Sarah's question: "The grass withers and flowers fade, but His word will stand forever."

For 700 years the people of Israel waited for the fulfillment of the words spoken through the prophet Isaiah saying, "For to us a child is born, to us a son is given, and the government will be on his shoulders. And he will be called Wonderful Counselor, Mighty God, Everlasting Father, Prince of Peace. Of the greatness of his government and peace there will be no end. He will reign on David's throne and over his kingdom, establishing and upholding it with justice and righteousness from that time on and forever. The zeal of the Lord Almighty will accomplish this" (Isa. 9:6-7).

Seven hundred years was a long time to wait. But God kept His promise. Unlike Sarah's flowers that faded away in a few days, God's Word stands eternal. It will not pass away. There are many promises (God's spoken words) in the Bible. Promises that will last forever. Read a few examples:

- "Everyone who calls on the name of the Lord will be saved" (Rom. 10:13).

- "My sheep listen to my voice; I know them, and they follow me" (Jn. 10:27).

- "So do not fear, for I am with you; do not be dismayed, for I am your God. I will strengthen you and help you; I will uphold you with my righteous right hand" (Isa. 41:10).

You can depend on God and His many good promises to His people. You can trust God's promises to you.

God's Promises, Your Life

1. How and when have you experienced any of the above promises?

2. What promise of God are you trusting Him for your specific need?

3. Write a prayer or draw a prayer picture based on what God spoke to you about today's verse, and your answers to the questions.

Rely on God's Word at
Psalm 119:140 • Matthew 5:18 • 1 Peter 1:25

STOPWATCH

Sun and moon stood
still in the heavens
at the glint of your
flying arrows, at the
lightning of your
flashing spear.

HABAKKUK 3:11

What activities have you participated in that were timed?

Meredith hurried through her timed math test. She breezed through the first questions and felt confident she would finish the test before the teacher's stopwatch sounded. But when she looked at the last few questions, the palms of her hands began to sweat. She thought to herself, *If only I could stop the timer, then I could finish the test!*

Like Meredith, moments occur when we run out of time and wish we could stop the clock. God did just that for the Israelites, and time stood still.

The Gibeonites (allies of Israel) got caught in a battle against five kings and their armies. They called out to the Israelites to help them. When Joshua, the leader of the Israelites, arrived with his army, the Lord told him not to worry. At the sight of Joshua and his army, men from the other armies panicked and started running away. The Israelites pursued them, but realized they were running out of daylight to fight

"Joshua said to the Lord in the presence of Israel: 'Sun, stand still over Gibeon, and you, moon, over the Valley of Aijalon.' So the sun stood still, and the moon stopped, till the nation avenged itself on its enemies … then Joshua returned with all Israel to the camp at Gilgal" (Josh. 10: 12b-15).

"The sun stopped in the middle of the sky and delayed going down about a full day. There has never been a day like it before or since, a day when the Lord listened to a mere human being. Surely the Lord was fighting for Israel!" (Josh. 10:13b-14).

This story reminds us that "with God all things are possible" (Mt. 19:26b). Even stopping time.

Your God of the Impossible

1. Meredith began to panic, thinking about not being able to finish her timed test. Describe a time when you had a similar feeling.

2. How could the story of stopping time help you trust God?

3. Write a prayer or draw a prayer picture based on today's scripture verse, devotional, and your answers to the questions.

Marvel at the God of the Impossible at
Matthew 17:20b • Matthew 19:26 • Mark 9:23

DAY 16

"I tell you," he replied, "if they keep quiet, the stones will cry out."

LUKE 19:40

STONES

What words do you say, or songs do you sing, to cheer on your favorite team?

Emanuel and Fredrick loved to attend their school's sports games. The upcoming Saturday night's football game was an important one. At the game they shouted encouragement, hoping their voices would carry across the field into the hearts of their team members.

As the star quarterback crossed the goal line, the crowd yelled, and the band played the school's victory song. Frederick and Emanuel cheered for their hero when he scored the winning touchdown.

The Bible tells stories about those who cheered for their champion, Jesus, even when others told them to keep silent. One day Jesus fulfilled prophecy by riding into Jerusalem on a donkey. The crowd around him shouted, "Blessed is the king who comes in the name of the LORD!" (Lk. 19:38). When the Pharisees asked Jesus to silence the crowd because people were shouting "Hosanna," He warned them if anybody tried to silence them, the stones would cry out (vs. 40).

Another story about praising God happened in a prison. The story began with Paul and Silas telling others about Jesus. As a result, they were stripped, beaten without mercy, and thrown into prison. The jailer knew if the prisoners escaped, he would be beaten, too. Or even killed.

The Bible story is miraculous:

> **About midnight Paul** and Silas were praying and singing hymns to God, and the other prisoners were listening to them. Suddenly there was such a violent earthquake that the foundations of the prison were shaken. At once all the prison

doors flew open, and everyone's chains came loose.

The jailer woke up, and when he saw the prison doors open, he drew his sword and was about to kill himself because he thought the prisoners had escaped.

But Paul shouted, "Don't harm yourself! We are all here!"

The jailer called for lights, rushed in and fell trembling before Paul and Silas. He then brought them out and asked, "Sirs, what must I do to be saved?" (Acts 16:25-30). ✦

Praising God in Good or Bad Times

1. There are many forms of praise and worship in the Bible: singing, dancing, clapping, bowing, and more. How and when do you praise and worship God?

2. Have you decided to praise the Lord during a difficult time? What happened?

3. Write a prayer or draw a prayer picture based on today's scripture verse, devotional, and your answers to the questions.

Be inspired to praise God at
Psalm 103 • Psalm 119:175 • Matthew 21:16 • 1 Peter 1:3

Open his eyes, Lord, so that he may see.

2 KINGS 6:17

GLASSES

What do you enjoy looking at?

Samuel found it difficult to read words on the chalkboard in his class-room. He also couldn't track the ball during baseball games. His mother thought he might need glasses, and an appointment with the eye doctor confirmed his eyesight had weakened. From the first time he wore his new glasses, he could tell a difference.

Just as Samuel couldn't see clearly in the natural world without glasses, we can't see into the spiritual world without faith. Faith is the "lens" we use to view what God sees.

In the Old Testament, Elisha and a young servant saw beyond the natural world into the spiritual world. The King of Aram was angry with Elisha, one of God's prophets, and sent an army to capture him.

"They went by night and surrounded the city. When the servant of the man of God got up and went out early the next morning, an army with chariots and horses had surrounded the city. 'Oh no, my lord! What shall we do?' the servant asked. 'Don't be afraid,' the prophet answered. 'Those who are with us are more than those who are with them'" (2 K 6:14-17).

Elisha saw into the spiritual world, and saw God's army ready to defend them.

Elisha and his servant saw God miraculously deliver Israel from the raiding army of Aram. (Read the whole story in 2 Kings 6:18-22.)

When problems seem too big to solve, as they did for Elisha's servant, we can put on the "spiritual glasses" of faith. We can ask God to show us how He's working in our situation.

Seeing God at Work

1. When have you felt something was too big for you to solve? How did the challenge work out?

_____

_____

_____

_____

2. Just like Samuel needed glasses to see clearly, we need faith to see our problems the way God does. How can you increase your "lens" of faith?

_____

_____

_____

_____

3. Write a prayer or draw a prayer picture based on today's scripture verse, devotional, and your answers to the questions.

Learn how to grow your faith at
Romans 10:17 • Hebrews 12:2 • I John 5:4-5

DAY 18

I am fearfully and wonderfully made.

PSALM 139:14

SPOON

What have you made with your hands?

Daniel's grandfather heated the forge in his blacksmith shop while his wide-eyed grandson held a piece of iron in his hands. Both Daniel and his grandfather felt the heat from the forge as it warmed the shop. When the forge reached the right temperature, Daniel's grandfather placed the iron into it. The iron began to glow red. Taking the hot metal out of the forge, Daniel's grandfather showed him how to pound the iron to form a spoon.

Finishing the spoon, Daniel exclaimed, "This is a good spoon! I am going to use it when I eat ice cream."

Like Daniel and his grandfather, most of us have made something with our hands. And like Daniel and his grandfather, we knew what we were making.

The first verse of Genesis says, "In the beginning God created the heavens and the earth." God began to create by saying, "Let there be light, and there was light" (vs 3). God's words were powerful. Every time God finished making something, He looked at it, and like Daniel, He said it was good.

After creating the world, God took dust in His hands and formed Adam, the first man. God gave Adam eyes to observe the beauty of His creation, and to see His face. He gave Adam ears to hear the sounds around him and to recognize His voice. He formed each part of Adam for specific purposes. Adam was a lifeless piece of clay until God breathed into Him. As God's breath flowed into Adam, he opened his eyes to God's face and heard Him say, "This is very good."

Just as Daniel and his grandfather formed his spoon for a unique purpose, God also created Adam for a reason: to know Him, love Him, and be loved by Him. God also created each one of us to know Him, love Him, and be loved by Him. And God says that we, His art pieces, are "very good"(vs. 31).

God Made You Unique

1. How does it feel to know God created you?

2. In what ways did God make you unique?

3. Write a prayer or draw a prayer picture based on today's scripture verse, devotional, and your answers to the questions.

Celebrate your uniqueness at
Genesis 1:27 • Isaiah 64:8 • Ephesians 2:19

DAY 19

LIGHT

You are the light of the world. A town built on a hill cannot be hidden. Neither do people light a lamp and put it under a bowl. Instead they put it on its stand, and it gives light to everyone in the house.

MATTHEW 5:14-15

Think of a time when you had trouble seeing in the dark.

"I can't see!" shouted Caleb. The black night closed in on him. The thunderstorm had knocked out the electricity in the house. Tonight, no lights peeked through the shadows. No lights shined from the neighbors' houses. Caleb missed the light.

Just as Caleb couldn't see without light, people who don't know Christ live in spiritual darkness and can't see the light of His truth. Jesus says as believers, we are like lights shining in the darkness. But what does that mean?

The Bible tells the story of how Paul became a light to the Gentiles. One day, on his way to destroy Christians in Damascus,

... a light from heaven flashed around him. He fell to the ground and heard a voice say to him, "Saul, Saul, why do you persecute me?"

"Who are you, Lord?" Saul asked.

"I am Jesus, whom you are persecuting," he replied. "Now get up and go into the city, and you will be told what you must do."

The men traveling with Saul stood speechless; they heard the sound, but didn't see anyone. Saul got up from the ground, but when he opened his eyes, he couldn't see anything. So the men led him by the hand into Damascus. For three days he was blind and did not eat or drink anything (Acts 9:3-9). ✦

Then God told Ananias, a Christian who lived nearby, to go to Paul and lay his hands on him and restore his sight. Ananias did so, and Paul regained his sight. "Saul spent several days with the disciples in Damascus and began to preach in the synagogues that Jesus is the Son of God" (Acts 9:19b-20).

Paul continued as a spiritual light to others as he shared the Gospel throughout many nations and cities. At times enemies beat him, threw him into prison, and persecuted him for sharing. Still, the light of Christ continued to shine through him, despite numerous attempts to stop him.

Shining In the Spiritual Darkness

1. Do you know someone who lives in spiritual darkness? How can you pray for this person?

2. When the time is right, how could you share Christ with this person?

3. Write a prayer or draw a prayer picture based on today's scripture verse, devotional, and your answers to the questions.

Recall how you were called into the light at
Isaiah 49:6 • Philippians 2:14-16 • 1 Peter 2:9

STARS

Has anyone broken a promise he or she made to you? What was it? How did you feel?

William excitedly ripped the wrapping paper off his gift. A broad smile burst across his face as he pulled out a telescope, a gift he'd hoped for all year. Looking into the night sky with his telescope, he saw the Big Dipper, Little Dipper, Hercules, and the Lion—a few of the constellations.

"Impressive!" exclaimed William.

A few thousand years ago, God told Abraham (a very old man who couldn't have children anymore) that his descendants would be as numerous as the stars in the sky. Trying to count all the stars in the universe would be like trying to count all the grains of sand on every shoreline. Impossible!

Imagine how surprised Abraham felt at hearing these words. Could it be possible that he and his wife Sarah would one day have children, and their descendants would be as numerous as the stars in the sky? Abraham held on to God's promise, and he and Sarah gave birth to a son named Isaac.

Every time we gaze into the sky and see all the stars, we're reminded that God keeps His promises, even when some of those promises seem impossible.

You and God's Promises

1. What promises of God are you holding on to?

_____

_____

_____

_____

2. What promises has God answered for you?

_____

_____

_____

_____

3. Write a prayer or draw a prayer picture based on today's scripture verse, devotional, and your answers to the questions.

Think about God's promises at
Numbers 23:19 • Deuteronomy 7:8-9 • Hebrew 6:13-15

DAY 21

MIRROR

Anyone who listens to the word but does not do what it says is like someone who looks at his face in a mirror and, after looking at himself, goes away and immediately forgets what he looks like.

JAMES 1:23-24

What do you most notice about yourself when you look in a mirror?

Sabrina could hardly believe she'd been invited to go to the mall with the most popular girls in school. Hurriedly, she put on her favorite outfit. Looking into the mirror, she wondered if she would fit in with these friends. The girls went to the stores where everybody shopped.

In the corner of the store, they found the latest ID bracelets. Eydie suggested they each take one and walk out of the store without paying for it. The bracelets were small, and easily slipped into their purses. But Sabrina didn't take one. She didn't want to steal and disobey God's Word. When the girls left the store, they teased Sabrina for being a coward.

Obeying God's Word is like looking into a mirror and remembering what you look like (Jas 1:23-24). In the Old Testament, Daniel didn't forget what he "looked like," even if it meant persecution. King Darius' administrators tricked him into making a law that no one could pray to anyone but to him. A lion's den awaited those who disobeyed. When Daniel heard the decree, he returned home, opened his windows, and prayed to God.

The administrators found Daniel praying, and told the king about him, knowing the decree couldn't be changed. "So, the king gave the order, and they brought Daniel and threw him into the lions' den. The king said to Daniel, 'May your God, whom you serve continually, rescue you!'" (Dan. 6:16b).

In the morning, the king arrived at the den and called out to Daniel, to check if God spared the young man's life. "Daniel answered, 'May the king live forever! My God sent his angel, and He shut the mouths of the lions. They have not hurt me, because I was found innocent in his sight. Nor have I ever done any wrong before you, Your Majesty'" (Dan. 6:21-22).

Daniel didn't "forget what he looked like" and obeyed God's command not to worship any other god (Ex. 20:3). Sabrina also remembered God's Word and obeyed when she chose not to steal (vs. 15).

Choosing to Do the Right Thing

1. When are you most likely to be like someone who "forgets what they look like?"

2. When do friends most likely influence your behavior? How can you choose to do the right thing?

3. Write a prayer or draw prayer picture based on today's scripture verse, devotional, and your answers to the questions.

Remember God's Word at
Psalm 119:105 • Proverbs 3:5-6 • Matthew 24:35

DAY 22

Cleanse me with hyssop, and I will be clean; wash me, and I will be whiter than snow.

PSALM 51:7

SNOW

What things remind you of being clean?

Seeing the newly fallen snow, Cassandra put on her boots and stepped outside to explore. She followed the rabbit tracks leading to the raspberry bushes and built a snowman. When Cassandra finished, she walked back to the house to warm up. Looking out a window, the sparkling snow caught her attention again, and she exclaimed, "It is so bright and clean looking!"

God desires us to be spiritually clean as white snow, to live free from sin.

In Psalm 51:7, David asked God to cleanse him from his sin so spiritually, he would be whiter than snow. He wanted the Lord to wash him with hyssop, a brush-like plant the Jewish people used in ceremonial cleansing practices.

Earlier, God named David a king of Israel. You might remember the story about David using a single stone to kill the giant, Goliath, and that God called David His friend. Even though David had a close friendship with God and knew God's will, he sinned. A sin is an action or thought that violates God's will. The Bible teaches us about sin (Ex 20:1-17).

In Psalm 51, David talked to God about his sin. David described his sin as always with him. He felt miserable because sin separated him from God. David asked God to extend mercy, blot out his transgressions, and cleanse away his sin. David confessed his sin and asked God to wash him whiter than snow. God heard David's prayer, forgave him, and thoroughly cleansed him from sin.

Sometimes we try to hide our sin and act like we did nothing wrong. This is never a good idea. Sin festers inside us and we feel awful. After we sin, we can talk to God about it, tell the truth, and ask Him to forgive us.

God assures us He is faithful and just. He forgives us when we confess and repent of our sin (1 Jn. 1:9). Freedom from sin feels like being clean. Even cleaner and fresher than white, sparkling snow.

Following David's Example

1. What were some times when you sinned?

   _____

   _____

   _____

2. Have you sinned and then felt like David? What did you do about it?

   _____

   _____

3. Write a prayer or draw a prayer picture based on today's scripture verse, devotional, and your answers to the questions.

   Experience the freedom of confession at
   Psalm 51 • Isaiah 1:18 • John 8:32

DAY 23

And whatever you do,
whether in word or
deed, do it all in
the name of the
Lord Jesus, giving
thanks to God the
Father through him.

COLOSSIANS 3:17

MONEY

If you had plenty of money, what would you buy?

Brandon shopped in an electronics store, and after looking at several new kinds of headphones, he decided to buy a set. Not only did the headphones cancel background noise, they would work well with his Bluetooth. Even more, they fit comfortably. Searching in his pants pockets, Brandon discovered he didn't have any money with him. He mistakenly left his wallet at home.

Brandon reminds me of two men in the Bible who also didn't have money when they met a beggar on the street. The story unfolded like this:

One day Peter and John were going up to the temple at the time of prayer—at three in the afternoon. Now a man who was lame from birth was being carried to the temple gate called Beautiful, where he was put every day to beg from those going into the temple courts.

When he saw Peter and John about to enter, he asked them for money. Peter looked straight at him, as did John. Then Peter said, "Look at us!" So, the man gave them his attention, expecting to get something from them. Then Peter said, "Silver or gold I do not have, but what I do have I give you. In the name of Jesus Christ of Nazareth, walk."

Taking him by the right hand, he [Peter] helped him up, and instantly the man's feet and ankles became strong. He jumped to his feet and began to walk. Then he went with them into the temple courts, walking and jumping, and praising God. When all the people saw him walking and praising God, they recognized him as the same man who used to sit begging at the temple gate called Beautiful, and they were filled with wonder and amazement at what had happened to him.

... When Peter saw this, he said to them: "Fellow Israelites, why does this surprise you? Why do you stare at us as if by our own power or godliness we had made this man walk? ... It is Jesus' name and the faith that comes through him that has completely healed him, as you can all see" (Acts 3:1-12, 16). ✦

Peter and John possessed something more powerful and helpful than money to give to the beggar. They had the name of Jesus.

Changing Your Viewpoint

1. How could this biblical story change the way you think about money?

2. How could you better understand and believe in the power of Jesus' name?

3. Write a prayer or draw a prayer picture based on today's scripture verse, devotional, and your answers to the questions.

Learn more about spiritual power at
Mark 16:17-18 • Acts 4:12 • Romans 14:11

SEEDS

For you have been born again, not of perishable seed, but of imperishable, through the living and enduring word of God.

I PETER 1:23

Have you ever tended a garden, plant, or yard? How did you take care of it?

Miranda eagerly planted seeds in anticipation of growing watermelons for the state fair. She watered the soil, pulled out weeds, and applied natural fertilizer to ensure the seeds would grow and mature into ripe, award-winning watermelons. Near the end of the summer, she was delighted to see many large, ripe watermelons on the vines.

When Jesus spoke about the Kingdom of God, He often told parables, simple stories that illustrate a moral or spiritual lesson. One day, when a large crowd gathered about Jesus, He told a parable about a farmer. Like Miranda, this farmer planted seeds.

Jesus began the parable by saying, "A farmer went out to sow his seed. As he was scattering the seed, some fell along the path; it was trampled on, and the birds ate it up. Some fell on rocky ground, and when it came up, the plants withered because they had no moisture. Other seed fell among thorns, which grew up with it and choked the plants. Still, other seed fell on good soil. It came up and yielded a crop, a hundred times more than was sown" (Lk. 8:5-8a).

When the disciples heard this parable, they asked Jesus to tell them what it meant. Jesus replied: "The seed is the word of God. Those along the path are the ones who hear, and then the devil comes and takes away the word from their hearts, so that they may not believe and be saved. Those on the rocky ground are the ones who receive the word with joy when they hear it, but they have no root. They believe for a while, but in the time of testing they fall away. The seed that fell among thorns stands for those who hear, but as they go on their way they are choked by life's worries, riches and pleasures, and they do not mature. But the seed on good soil stands for those with a noble and good heart, who hear the word, retain it, and by persevering produce a crop" (Lk. 8:11b-15).

The watermelon seeds that Miranda planted needed good soil and care to grow into ripe melons. God's word also needs a fertile place to grow and mature in our own livess.

The Seeds of God's Word

1. How can you nurture the words of God you've heard?

    _____

    _____

    _____

2. Read again Luke 8:1-12. How can you apply this parable to your understanding and practice of God's Word?

    _____

    _____

    _____

3. Write a prayer or draw a prayer picture based on today's scripture verse, devotional, and your answers to the questions.

> Consider the power of spiritual seeds at
> Isaiah 40:8 • Matthew 13:31-32 • Corinthians 9:6

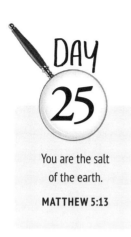

DAY 25

You are the salt
of the earth.

MATTHEW 5:13

SALT

What food would you miss if it wasn't salty?

Cassandra chose salt as her research project at school. She liked pickles, potato chips, popcorn, and other salty foods. It surprised her to learn salt was an antiseptic, preservative, and flavor-enhancer. Plus at one time, salt used to pay people for their work. The word "salary" originated from using salt as a form of money.

As Cassandra studied salt, she remembered the words of Jesus: "You are the salt of the earth. But if the salt loses its saltiness, how can it be made salty again? It is no longer good for anything, except to be thrown out and trampled underfoot" (Mt. 5:13).

Cassandra asked God to help her be the "salt of the earth." She thought of several Bible characters who were "salty." Paul evangelized many people. Samuel spoke God's truth when Israel didn't obey God. David worshipped God with all his heart.

As Cassandra reflected on these lives, she realized these individuals took actions that others did not, helping people persevere in the Faith. They were "salt of the earth."

As Cassandra prayed, she thought of a girl in school who students frequently bullied. She smiled as she sensed God showed her how to be "like salt" to this classmate, and to the others.

Cassandra also looked up verses about how to be "salt" in interactions with her classmates. She found these:

"Salt is good, but if it loses its saltiness, how can you make it salty again? Have salt among yourselves and be at peace with each other" (Mk. 9:50).

"Let your conversation be always full of grace, seasoned with salt, so that you may know how to answer everyone"(Col. 4:6).

Becoming "Salty" in Your Life

1. Read again the verses that Cassandra found. What did you hear the Lord saying to you through these verses?

2. Ask the Lord to show you how to apply these verses to your life. As you pray and reflect, do you sense the Lord showing you anything? If so, what is it?

3. Write a prayer or draw a prayer picture based on today's scripture verse, devotional, and your answers to the questions.

Practice actions that make you "salty" at
Romans 10:15 • I Corinthians 13:3-8 • Hebrews 10:35-36

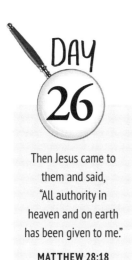

Then Jesus came to them and said, "All authority in heaven and on earth has been given to me."

MATTHEW 28:18

BADGE

Do you know anyone who wears a badge? What authority do they have?

Angela noticed the heavy traffic flow as she and her friends walked to the football game. Drivers impatiently honked their horns. As the girls approached the busy intersection, they wondered how they would get across the street. Angela noticed a police officer and asked him to help them. The officer put up his hand, and the cars stopped. The girls safely walked across the street.

Why would drivers stop their cars and pedestrians step into a busy street when a man stepped into the traffic flow? Because they understood the authority in the position of a police officer. His badge was an outward sign of his authority.

Peter and John, two disciples of Jesus, and a beggar all witnessed the power and authority of Jesus. As Peter and John walked to the temple to pray, they saw a lame man begging outside the building. "When he saw Peter and John about to enter, he asked them for money. Peter looked straight at him, as did John. Then Peter said, 'Look at us!' So the man gave them his attention, expecting to get something from them. Then Peter said, 'Silver or gold I do not have, but what I do have I give you. In the name of Jesus Christ of Nazareth, walk.' Taking him by the right hand, he helped him up, and instantly the man's feet and ankles became strong. He jumped to his feet and began to walk" (Acts 3:3-7).

Angela and her friends saw the traffic stop because a police officer held the authority to halt it. Similarly, a lame beggar recovered because Peter also wore a "badge," the authority of Jesus to heal the sick. Peter explained to the crowd, "By faith in the name of Jesus, this man whom you see and know was made strong. It is Jesus' name and the faith that comes through Him that has completely healed him, as you can all see" (Acts 3:16).

God's Authority for You

1. How can the authority of Jesus heal the sick?

2. Have you seen God's authority in your life?

3. Write a prayer or draw a prayer picture based on today's scripture verse, devotional, and your answers to the questions.

Read how the name of Jesus creates authority:
John 14:13-14 • John 20:31 • Colossians 3:17

RUNNING SHOES

> Therefore, since we are surrounded by such a great cloud of witnesses, let us throw off everything that hinders and the sin that so easily entangles. And let us run with perseverance the race marked out for us.
>
> **HEBREWS 12:1**

Have you ever participated in a competition? How did you prepare to compete?

William spent months preparing for today's race. As he put on his running shoes, he thought about how many times he'd felt tempted to play his favorite video games or just hang out and do nothing, instead of attending practices. At times, William thought he couldn't run one more step; it felt like his lungs would heave out of his chest. It would've been easy for him not to practice, and he wondered if all those hours really would make any difference.

Even though it was chilly the morning of the race, William decided to wear his lightest running gear. He knew any extra weight could slow him down. As William approached the starting line, he threw off his warm-up suit, positioned himself, and waited for the signal to start. "On your mark. Get set. Go!" As William's legs pumped, the other runners fell behind him. His steady, accelerating pace carried him across the finish line in first place. His faithful practicing paid off.

Paul, who wrote the book of Hebrews, compared the Christian life to a race and explained how to run it well. First, we should throw off anything hindering us. Sometimes doubt, stress, or disappointments weigh us down. Second, we cast off sin. We do this by confessing our wrongs and asking for forgiveness. Third, we persevere and not give up (Heb. 12:1).

William persevered through his practices, even though he felt like quitting. We persist in our faith by continuing to make the right choices, even when they are hard. The apostle Paul's life exemplified someone who ran the race well. He endured beatings, imprisonment, shipwrecks, persecution, and hunger as he proclaimed the Good News of Jesus Christ. His faithfulness modeled how to run the race marked out of us.

Running Your Race with Jesus

1. How do you prepare to run your race as a Christian?

2. What could you change to help run your race better? How can you make that change?

3. Write a prayer or draw a prayer picture based on today's scripture verse, devotional, and your answers to the questions.

Check out the need for endurance at
Ephesians 6:10-18 • Hebrews 10:35-36 • James 1:12

DAY 28

GIFTS

There are different kinds of gifts, but the same Spirit distributes them. There are different kinds of service, but the same Lord.

1 CORINTHIANS 12:4-5

Have you ever received a special gift? What was it? Who gave it to you?

Maria's father handed her a gift. The artistically wrapped box didn't rattle as she shook it, hoping to discover what might be inside. She methodically unwrapped it and excitedly found a picture of the bicycle she'd asked for. Setting the box on the table, Maria rushed to her father, hugging him and exclaiming, "Thank you, thank you!"

Like friends and family, God gives us gifts too. They are spiritual gifts. A spiritual gift is a unique expression of God's grace, given to each believer, to help strengthen and encourage one another in our faith.

In 1 Corinthians 12:8-10, Paul mentioned the gifts of wisdom, knowledge, faith, healing, working of miracles, prophecy, distinguishing spirits, speaking in tongues, and the interpretation of tongues. In Romans, Paul said we use our spiritual gifts according to our faith. Among those gifts are serving, giving, showing mercy, and encouraging one another (Rom, 12:6-8).

Many individuals in the Bible used their spiritual gifts. For example, Barnabas encouraged people. Stephen exercised faith and served others. Paul evangelized and worked miracles.

Just as Maria asked her father for a bicycle, Paul encouraged all believers to ask God for His spiritual gifts. We can use them to help others grow in their faith. God loves to give us these gifts!

Receiving Your Spiritual Gifts

1. Have you asked God for your spiritual gifts? If not, you can ask Him now. If you already know your spiritual gifts, what are they?

2. Write about a time when you used your spiritual gifts.

3. Write a prayer or draw a prayer picture based on today's scripture verse, devotional, and your answers to the questions.

Prepare to receive God's good gifts at
Romans 12:5-6 • James 1:17 • 1 Peter 4:10

DAY 29

How precious
to me are your
thoughts, God!
How vast is the sum
of them! Were I
to count them, they
would outnumber
the grains of sand …

PSALM 139:17-18

SAND

What do you think about yourself?

The contest was impossible, I mean who could guess how many grains of sand were in the jar. Blake tried to figure it out by counting the number of grains of sand in a teaspoon and the number of teaspoons in the jar. It didn't take him long to realize counting the grains was a lost cause.

God tells us that His thoughts towards us are more in number than the grains of sand, not in a jar, but in the universe.

Blake disliked the way his ears stuck out, the way his large nose seemed to cover his face, and the way the kids treated him at school. Most of all, he disliked that he was not athletic. Although he did well in school, he thought of himself as being a loser, and envied many of his classmates.

Blake reminds me of a young man named Gideon. Like Blake, Gideon did not think very much of himself. Gideon lived in Israel a long time ago. He and his family lived in fear of the Midianites, dangerous people who were harassing and hurting them. Every time Gideon's community was about to harvest their wheat, which was their food and livelihood, the Midianites stole or destroyed all of it. Because he was afraid of them, Gideon was hiding by himself, milling some wheat in secret, when an angel of the Lord spoke to him: "You are strong. Go and save Israel from the power of Midian. I am sending you."

At first, Gideon could not believe what he was hearing. Gideon told the angel that he was weak, but the angel said, "The LORD is with you, mighty warrior" (Judges 6:12). Gideon still didn't believe it. "How can I save Israel?" he asked. "My clan is the weakest in Manasseh, and I am the least in my family" (Judges 6:15).

Firmly and kindly, the LORD continued to tell Gideon what His thoughts and plans were for him. "I will be with you, and you will strike down all of the Midianites, leaving none alive" (Judges 6:16). Gideon continued to listen to the plans and thoughts that God had for him--and as he heard, he began to believe them. God gave him a stunning victory.

The thoughts that Gideon had about himself were different than the ones that God had about him.

God's Thoughts about You

1. What thoughts do you think God has about you?

2. How could those thoughts influence your actions or the way you see yourself?

3. Write a prayer or draw a prayer picture based on today's scripture verse, devotion, and your answers to the questions.

Additional Reading:
Deuteronomy 31:8 • 1 John 3:2 • Zephaniah 3:17

DAY 30

...I have set my rainbow in the clouds, and it will be the sign of the covenant between me and the earth.

GENESIS 9:12-13

RAINBOW

Have you ever kept a promise? What was it?

Jeremy disappointedly returned to class after recess, muttering to himself, "A promise is a promise, and Michael broke his." His friend, Michael, agreed to play tag football with him, but decided to play basketball with other friends instead.

Like Jeremy, many of us experience broken promises. Yet, promises don't exist just between individuals. They also can be forged and broken between groups and countries. Even God makes promises, but He never breaks them.

In the Bible, agreements or promises between two people were called covenants. At one point in the Old Testament, the earth filled with wickedness, except for Noah, a godly man. God instructed Noah to build an ark because He would flood the earth and destroy life. Noah faithfully built the enormous boat for himself, his family, and two each of the earth's animals, despite people ridiculing him.

At the appointed time, it began to rain. It rained for 40 days, and water covered the earth, as God said. After the water receded, God told Noah and his family to exit the boat, along with the animals. Then God said to Noah and his sons, "'I now establish my covenant with you and with your descendants ... Never again will all life be destroyed by the waters of a flood; never again will there be a flood to destroy the earth.' And God said, 'This is the sign of the covenant, I am making between

you and me and every living creature with you, a covenant for all generations to come: I have set my rainbow in the clouds, and it will be the
sign of the covenant between me and the earth'" (Gen. 9:8-13).

The rainbow reminds us of God's faithfulness to His covenant with us.

God and His Promises

1. Name some of the promises you've found in the Bible.

2. Which one means the most to you? Why?

3. Write a prayer or draw a prayer picture based on today's scripture
   verse, devotional, and your answers to the questions.

Rest assured about God's promises and faithfulness at
Deuteronomy 7:9 • 2 Timothy 2:13 • Hebrews 10:23

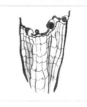

CREATE
YOUR OWN
DEVOTIONS

Now that you've
finished this devotional, you can
practice seeing everyday objects as
God's reminders of His relationship
with you. Use the outline on the
following pages to create your
own daily devotions.

YOUR
1
DEVOTION

YOUR ORDINARY THING

DRAW YOUR ORDINARY THING

YOUR VERSE

_____

_____

_____

_____

YOUR STORY/MEMORY

_____

_____

_____

_____

_____

_____

_____

_____

_____

BIBLE STORY

YOUR QUESTIONS.

YOUR ORDINARY THING

DRAW YOUR ORDINARY THING

YOUR VERSE

_____

_____

_____

_____

YOUR STORY/MEMORY

_____

_____

_____

_____

_____

_____

_____

_____

BIBLE STORY

YOUR QUESTIONS

ABOUT THE AUTHOR

Kathleen Trock-Molhoek has a passion for children and adults to know God as their Father. She is the founder of Pebbles and Stones (www.Pebblesandstones.com), a ministry that brings the gospel to children and adults through biblical storytelling, listening, journaling, sharing, and praying in an intergenerational setting. Her teaching model is used in 50 countries. She is the author of *Hiding Places, I Love to Pray, God Speaks,* and *Kids Love to Pray Too.* She and her husband, Dan, live in Ada, MI.

Pebbles & Stones

P.O. Box 625
Ada, MI 49301

Bringing generations together to experience God's love

Pebbles and Stones is a Christian teaching ministry that equips believers to facilitate intergenerational gatherings with a focus on hearing God's voice. We want to see followers of Jesus all over the world gathering together to experience God's love in profoundly tangible ways. Our goal is to provide believers with a teaching model they can use anywhere — we call it Pebbles and Stones.

The model has been used in over 50 countries. Church leaders, parents, youth leaders, Bible school teachers, grandparents, and others attend our trainings to learn how using this inter-generational model can meet the spiritual, emotional, and physical of those around us. If you were to participate in a Pebbles and Stones meeting, you would see the generations giving to and receiving from each other. In this organic setting, personal growth and intimacy with God and others are experienced.

Trainings are usually hosted by non-profit organizations and churches. To host a training or to learn more about the model contact Kathleen Trock-Molhoek at:

info@pebblesandstones.com
and visit our website at
www.PebblesandStones.com

Topics covered in the training include
Hearing God's Voice, Healing Hearts,
and Discipline Versus Punishment.

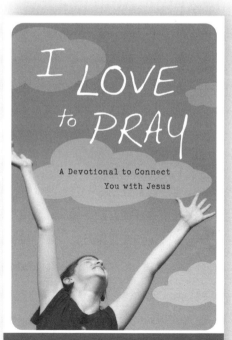